"I Need You There!"
Sang The King

To

_____

From

_____

Date

_____

This children's coloring book and storybook is based on the true story of Dean Braxton dying for 1 hour and 45 minutes and going to Heaven.

"I Need You There!" Sang The King

Coloring Book and Storybook

"I Need You There!" Sang The King | Coloring Book and Storybook

Moments In Heaven Series:
Book 5

ISBN 978-0-9978372-4-7

Printed in the United States of America

www.DeanBraxton.com

"I Need You There!" Sang The King
Coloring Book and Storybook

DEDICATION

Dedicated to my younger grandchildren: Ayanna Nicole Braxton, Gabrielle Angela Wright, Johnathan Joseph Wright, Chariot Eliana Braxton, Brooklyn Kennedy Braxton, and Javelin Elizabeth Braxton.

As I left Earth to go to Heaven,

all I could see

was an amazing,

bright light shining at me!

I entered Heaven,

and the flowers sang,

"Welcome! Welcome!

We are glad you came!"

The joy! The joy!

As they sang to me,

"This way! This way!

To the King of kings!"

The birds even sang as I walked the path,

"Hurry! Hurry! To The King at last!"

I can still hear

all the melodies.

"The King is waiting for you!”

sang the trees.

There, it was normal

to watch them dance.

"Who danced?" You ask.

Just look! The grass!

The flowers on the sides

of the path belted out,

"He's going to see

The King right now!"

Then the trees sang

as their arms swung,

"It's time to meet

the Holy One!"

As I walked to the end of the path,

I saw

the King of Glory

who left me in awe!

What a sight

for my heart to see!

So, what did I do?

I fell to my knees.

What was I thinking,

down on my knees?

The cross!

The cross...

You did This for

What else could I do

as He stood before me?

I sang! I sang!

Because I was free.

I worshiped! I worshiped!

I worshiped my Lord!

And so did the water.

We never got bored.

Look there!

The mountains rolled and sang a few things.

A spectacular summit bowed

to a more spectacular King!

And above? Just look!

The thunder! The lightning!

They sang, and laughed,

and never were frightening.

Then, I stared at The King.

I'm complete! No lack!

He sang, "It is not your time.

Go back...

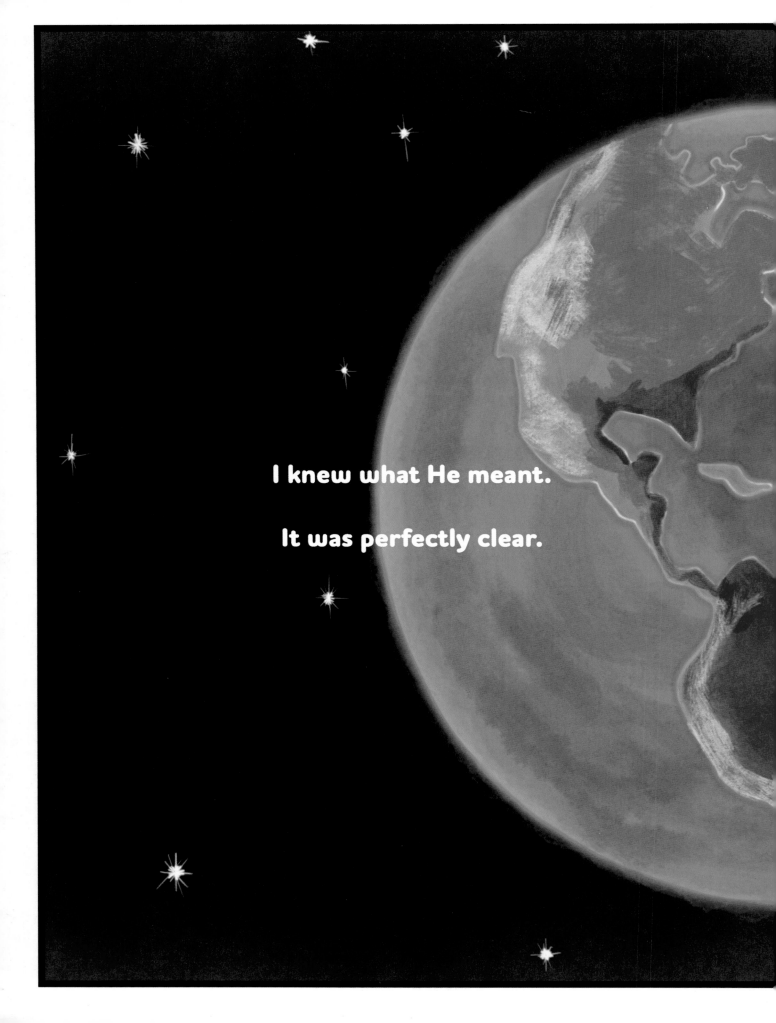

I knew what He meant.

It was perfectly clear.

"I need you there, on Earth," sang The King,

"more than I need you here!"

Now, back on Earth,
Jesus wants me to say,

He loves you
and has purpose for you
HERE
every day.

Dean Braxton died for 1 hour and 45 minutes and was miraculously prayed back to life. During his experience in Heaven, he was told by Jesus, "No, it is not your time. Go back!" Dean shares his story, emphasizing how much God loves each and every one of us. His testimony has led thousands to give their hearts to the Lord. Dean is a licensed minister and has been in ministry for over 20 years. He is happily married to his wife, Marilyn, with whom he has shared over 30 years of marriage. Dean loves to color, and his favorite color is yellow!

Sarah Braxton grew up in Gig Harbor, Washington, in a big family of eight with lots of family pets. She even had a bunny named Sadie who could walk on a leash and enjoyed looking out the window whenever riding in the car! She has loved to draw, doodle, and paint for as long as she can remember. Sarah doesn't have a favorite color because she likes so many of them. If she had to choose one, it would be purple! She resides in Virginia with her husband, Gabriel; two young daughters, Chariot and Javelin; and her fluffy dog, Bear.

Dean, the author, and Sarah, the illustrator, want you to know that Jesus loves you. You have a God-given plan and purpose on this Earth. Never forget that as long as you have air in your lungs, He is excited to do life with you right HERE on this planet.

"For God so loved the world that He gave His only begotten Son, that who-ever believes in Him should not perish but have everlasting life. For God did not send His Son into the world to condemn the world, but that the world through Him might be saved." John 3:16-17

Do you need help finding your path to Jesus? Ask your parent or guardian, visit your local church, or go to:

www.DeanBraxton.com

Made in the USA
Columbia, SC
28 March 2023

14436402R00027